RECYCLING

BY HARRIET BRUNDLE

PLANET EARTH HELPERS

BookLife
PUBLISHING

©2020
BookLife Publishing Ltd.
King's Lynn
Norfolk PE30 4LS

A catalogue record for this book is available from the British Library.

ISBN: 978-1-78637-993-1

Written by:
Harriet Brundle

Edited by:
Emilie Dufresne

Designed by:
Jasmine Pointer

All facts, statistics, web addresses and URLs in this book were verified as valid and accurate at time of writing. No responsibility for any changes to external websites or references can be accepted by either the author or publisher.

IMAGE CREDITS

All images are courtesy of Shutterstock.com, unless otherwise specified. With thanks to Getty Images, Thinkstock Photo and iStockphoto. Front Cover – VectorShow. 5 – Eduard Radu. 7 – maryliflower. 8 – Aphasara, SmallSnail, StockSmartStart. 9 – Inspiring, MicroOne. 11 – vladwel. 13 – Dukesn, Katy Flaty, StockSmartStart. 16 – StockSmartStart, Roi and Roi. 18 – YevO, NotionPic, LynxVector, angkrit. 19 – AVA Bitter. 21 – edel.

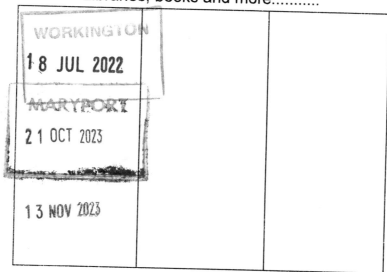

CONTENTS

Words that look like **this** can be found in the glossary on page 24.

RUBBISH

We all throw things away every day. It may be a wrapper from something you've eaten, a toy you don't use anymore or something which has broken. All of these things become rubbish.

Hi! My name is Priya Plastic.

The rubbish you throw away must go somewhere. Lots of rubbish goes into landfill. A landfill site is a huge hole in the ground where **waste** is dumped.

Landfill is not good for our planet.

RECYCLING

Recycling is when the things we throw away are made into something which can be used again, rather than being dumped.

The recycling **symbol** looks like this.

Lots of everyday items can be recycled using different **techniques**. If you see the recycling symbol on anything you're throwing away, it means it can be recycled.

WHY IS RECYCLING IMPORTANT?

It's important for all of us to know what can be recycled.
This is so that we can reduce the amount of waste that is made.

RECYCLING

WASTE

Check every item for the recycling symbol.

Lots of the ways we get rid of waste cause **pollution**, which is bad for the **environment**. The more we can recycle, the better it is for our planet.

Pollution is bad for everyone.

WHERE DO I RECYCLE?

Hi, I'm Riccardo Recycling. You can put your recycling in me.

Lots of homes now have special bins that are only for items that can be recycled. Before throwing something away, check whether it can be recycled and then put it in the correct bin.

There are also recycling centres and banks, such as bottle banks, where you can take your recycling. You might notice them in and around your local area and at supermarkets.

Your local bottle bank might look like this.

HOW DOES RECYCLING WORK?

Hi, I'm Priya and I'm being recycled.

Hi Priya, I'm Riccardo. It's nice to meet you!

After you have thrown your recycling into the bin, it is collected every few weeks by a lorry. The recycling is then taken to a centre, where it is unloaded.

The recycling is sorted and anything that has been recycled incorrectly is taken away. The recycling moves along on **conveyor belts** and is sorted into groups, such as glass and plastic.

The sorted items can then be recycled. Some **materials**, such as plastics, are melted and made into something new. Paper is washed and turned into **pulp**. It is then rolled out to make new paper.

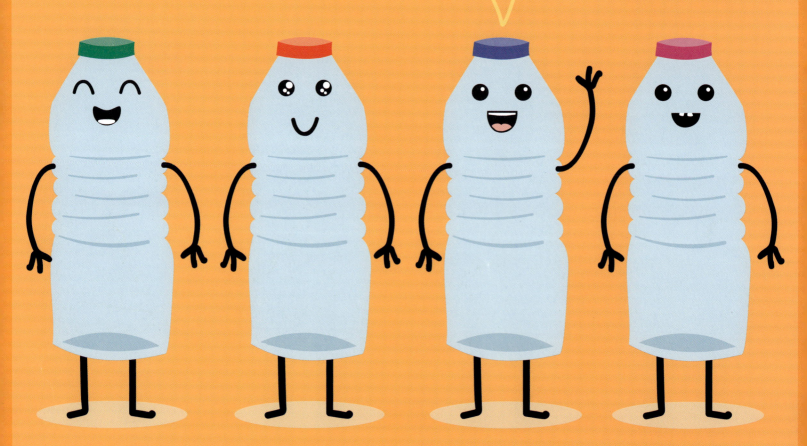

We're going to become something new.

Some things can be made into new versions of themselves. For example, paper can be used to make paper and glass can be used to make glass. Old plastic items can be used to make packaging, bottles and clothes.

WHAT CAN I RECYCLE?

Lots of different items can be recycled. Let's take a look at some of them.

SOME TYPES OF PLASTIC

PAPER AND CARDBOARD

GLASS JARS AND BOTTLES

DRINK CANS

FOOD TINS

Always check which items can be put in me, and which items need to go to a special recycling centre.

Before you put anything in your recycling bin, you or your parents will need to wash out any food or **residue** left on the things you are recycling.

You can squash me to make more room for other recyclable items.

WHAT CAN'T I RECYCLE?

Unfortunately, there are still lots of items we use every day that can't be included in our home recycling.
Some of these things are:

- Crisp packets and plastic bags
- Dirty pizza boxes and polystyrene containers
- Toothpaste tubes

Don't put any of those items in me. Check your local recycling centre to see if any of these items can be recycled there.

Wet wipes are bad for our environment because we only use them once and we can't recycle them.

Although we only use them once, most wet wipes and nappies cannot be recycled. Each one that is used goes straight into the waste.

19

REDUCE, REUSE, RECYCLE

Each day, it's important to try to reduce the amount of rubbish you're throwing away. Before you use something, think about what it is made of and if it can be recycled.

If you must throw something away, recycle when possible.

Reuse items when you can. Before you throw something away, ask yourself if you or someone you know could use the item for something else.

HOW CAN I HELP?

Always make sure you put your rubbish in a bin. When you throw something away, check for the recycling symbol or ask an adult if it can be recycled.

We work really well together, Priya!

You're the best, Riccardo.

Tell your friends and family how important it is to recycle. If you don't have a recycling bin at home or at school, speak to an adult about getting one.

GLOSSARY

CONVEYOR BELTS   moving bands that move things from one place to another

ENVIRONMENT   the natural world

MATERIALS   things from which objects are made

POLLUTION   harmful and poisonous things being added to an environment

PULP   a soft, wet material

RESIDUE   a small amount of something left on something else

SYMBOL   a thing that is used as a sign of something else

TECHNIQUES   ways of doing something

WASTE   things left over that are no longer needed

INDEX